Bugs in My...

I See
Moths

By Julia Jaske

I see a moth.

I see a moth flying.

4 I see a moth hiding.

I see a moth exploring.

I see a white moth.

I see a green moth.

I see a brown moth.

I see a colorful moth.

I see a moth climbing.

I see a moth resting.

I see a moth collecting.

I see a moth saying hello!

Word List

moth

flying

hiding

exploring

white

green

brown

colorful

climbing

resting

collecting

saying

hello

I see a moth.

I see a moth flying.

I see a moth hiding.

I see a moth exploring.

I see a white moth.

I see a green moth.

I see a brown moth.

I see a colorful moth.

I see a moth climbing.

I see a moth resting.

I see a moth collecting.

I see a moth saying hello!

CHERRY BLOSSOM PRESS

Published in the United States of America by Cherry Lake Publishing Group
Ann Arbor, Michigan
www.cherrylakepublishing.com

Book Designer: Melinda Millward

Photo Credits: ©Creative bee Maja/Shutterstock.com, front cover, 1; ©Matee Nuserm/
Shutterstock.com, back cover, 14; ©Foto by KKK/Shutterstock.com, 2; ©Cathy Keifer/
Shutterstock.com, 3; ©Henrik Larsson/Shutterstock.com, 4; ©Jean Landry/Shutterstock.com, 5;
©Barry and Carole Bowden/Shutterstock.com, 6; ©Amy C Anderson/Shutterstock.com, 7; ©Simon
Kovacic/Shutterstock.com, 8; ©Mark Brandon/Shutterstock.com, 9; ©Matthias Brix/Shutterstock.
com, 10; ©Davide Bonora/Shutterstock.com, 11; ©Les Weber/Shutterstock.com, 12; ©Manjith
Munnamkutty/Shutterstock.com, 13

Cherry Blossom Press is an imprint of Cherry Lake Publishing Group.

Library of Congress Cataloging-in-Publication Data

Names: Jaske, Julia, author.
Title: I see moths / by Julia Jaske.
Description: Ann Arbor, Michigan : Cherry Lake Publishing, 2022. | Series: Bugs in my backyard |
    Audience: Grades K-1
Identifiers: LCCN 2021036411 (print) | LCCN 2021036412 (ebook) | ISBN 9781534198906
    (paperback) | ISBN 9781668905807 (ebook) | ISBN 9781668901489 (pdf)
Subjects: LCSH: Moths—Juvenile literature.
Classification: LCC QL544.2 .J374 2022 (print) | LCC QL544.2 (ebook) | DDC 595.78—dc23
LC record available at https://lccn.loc.gov/2021036411
LC ebook record available at https://lccn.loc.gov/2021036412

Cherry Lake Publishing Group would like to acknowledge the work of the Partnership for 21st
Century Learning, a Network of Battelle for Kids. Please visit http://www.battelleforkids.org/
networks/p21 for more information.

Printed in the United States of America
Corporate Graphics